ANT

SOPHOCLES

Translated by
F. STORR

ANTIGONE

ARGUMENT

Antigone, daughter of Oedipus, the late king of Thebes, in defiance of Creon who rules in his stead, resolves to bury her brother Polyneices, slain in his attack on Thebes. She is caught in the act by Creon's watchmen and brought before the king. She justifies her action, asserting that she was bound to obey the eternal laws of right and wrong in spite of any human ordinance. Creon, unrelenting, condemns her to be immured in a rock-hewn chamber. His son Haemon, to whom Antigone is betrothed, pleads in vain for her life and threatens to die with her. Warned by the seer Teiresias Creon repents him and hurries to release Antigone from her rocky prison. But he is too late: he finds lying side by side Antigone who had hanged herself and Haemon who also has perished by his own hand. Returning to the palace he sees within the dead body of his queen who on learning of her son's death has stabbed herself to the heart.

DRAMATIS PERSONAE

ANTIGONE and ISMENE—daughters
    of Oedipus and sisters of Polyneices
and Eteocles.
CREON, King of Thebes.
HAEMON, Son of Creon, betrothed to
    Antigone.
EURYDICE, wife of Creon.
TEIRESIAS, the prophet.
CHORUS, of Theban elders.
A WATCHMAN
A MESSENGER
A SECOND MESSENGER

ANTIGONE and ISMENE before the Palace gates.

ANTIGONE
Ismene, sister of my blood and heart,
See'st thou how Zeus would in our lives
    fulfill

The weird of Oedipus, a world of woes!
For what of pain, affliction, outrage,
    shame,
Is lacking in our fortunes, thine and mine?
And now this proclamation of today
Made by our Captain-General to the
    State,
What can its purport be? Didst hear and
    heed,
Or art thou deaf when friends are banned
    as foes?

ISMENE
To me, Antigone, no word of friends
Has come, or glad or grievous, since we
    twain
Were reft of our two brethren in one day
By double fratricide; and since i' the night
Our Argive leaguers fled, no later news
Has reached me, to inspirit or deject.

ANTIGONE
I know 'twas so, and therefore summoned
    thee
Beyond the gates to breathe it in thine ear.

ISMENE

What is it? Some dark secret stirs thy
    breast.

ANTIGONE

What but the thought of our two brothers
    dead,
The one by Creon graced with funeral
    rites,
The other disappointed? Eteocles
He hath consigned to earth (as fame
    reports)
With obsequies that use and wont ordain,
So gracing him among the dead below.
But Polyneices, a dishonored corse,
(So by report the royal edict runs)
No man may bury him or make lament—
Must leave him tombless and unwept, a
    feast
For kites to scent afar and swoop upon.
Such is the edict (if report speak true)
Of Creon, our most noble Creon, aimed
At thee and me, aye me too; and anon
He will be here to promulgate, for such
As have not heard, his mandate; 'tis in
    sooth
No passing humor, for the edict says

Whoe'er transgresses shall be stoned to
    death.
So stands it with us; now 'tis thine to show
If thou art worthy of thy blood or base.

ISMENE
But how, my rash, fond sister, in such case
Can I do anything to make or mar?

ANTIGONE
Say, wilt thou aid me and abet? Decide.

ISMENE
In what bold venture? What is in thy
    thought?

ANTIGONE
Lend me a hand to bear the corpse away.

ISMENE
What, bury him despite the interdict?

ANTIGONE
My brother, and, though thou deny him,
    thine
No man shall say that I betrayed a
    brother.

ISMENE

Wilt thou persist, though Creon has
  forbid?

ANTIGONE

What right has he to keep me from
  my own?

ISMENE

Bethink thee, sister, of our father's fate,
Abhorred, dishonored, self-convinced
  of sin,
Blinded, himself his executioner.
Think of his mother-wife (ill sorted names)
Done by a noose herself had twined to
  death
And last, our hapless brethren in one day,
Both in a mutual destiny involved,
Self-slaughtered, both the slayer and the
  slain.
Bethink thee, sister, we are left alone;
Shall we not perish wretchedest of all,
If in defiance of the law we cross
A monarch's will?—weak women, think of
  that,
Not framed by nature to contend
  with men.
Remember this too that the stronger rules;

We must obey his orders, these or worse.
Therefore I plead compulsion and entreat
The dead to pardon. I perforce obey
The powers that be. 'Tis foolishness, I
    ween,
To overstep in aught the golden mean.

ANTIGONE
I urge no more; nay, wert thou willing still,
I would not welcome such a fellowship.
Go thine own way; myself will bury him.
How sweet to die in such employ, to rest,

—

Sister and brother linked in love's
    embrace—
A sinless sinner, banned awhile on earth,
But by the dead commended; and
    with them
I shall abide for ever. As for thee,
Scorn, if thou wilt, the eternal laws of
    Heaven.

ISMENE
I scorn them not, but to defy the State
Or break her ordinance I have no skill.

ANTIGONE
A specious pretext. I will go alone

To lap my dearest brother in the grave.

ISMENE
My poor, fond sister, how I fear for thee!

ANTIGONE
O waste no fears on me; look to thyself.

ISMENE
At least let no man know of thine intent,
But keep it close and secret, as will I.

ANTIGONE
O tell it, sister; I shall hate thee more
If thou proclaim it not to all the town.

ISMENE
Thou hast a fiery soul for numbing work.

ANTIGONE
I pleasure those whom I would liefest
    please.

ISMENE
If thou succeed; but thou art doomed to
    fail.

ANTIGONE
When strength shall fail me, yes, but not
 before.

ISMENE
But, if the venture's hopeless, why essay?

ANTIGONE
Sister, forbear, or I shall hate thee soon,
And the dead man will hate thee too, with
 cause.
Say I am mad and give my madness rein
To wreck itself; the worst that can befall
Is but to die an honorable death.

ISMENE
Have thine own way then; 'tis a mad
 endeavor,
Yet to thy lovers thou art dear as ever.
[Exeunt]

CHORUS
(Str. 1)
Sunbeam, of all that ever dawn upon
Our seven-gated Thebes the brightest ray,
O eye of golden day,
How fair thy light o'er Dirce's fountain
 shone,

Speeding upon their headlong homeward
    course,
Far quicker than they came, the Argive
    force;
Putting to flight
The argent shields, the host with
    scutcheons white.
Against our land the proud invader came
To vindicate fell Polyneices' claim.
Like to an eagle swooping low,
On pinions white as new fall'n snow.
With clanging scream, a horsetail plume
    his crest,
The aspiring lord of Argos onward
    pressed.

(Ant. 1)
Hovering around our city walls he waits,
His spearmen raven at our seven gates.
But ere a torch our crown of towers could
    burn,
Ere they had tasted of our blood,
    they turn
Forced by the Dragon; in their rear
The din of Ares panic-struck they hear.
For Zeus who hates the braggart's boast
Beheld that gold-bespangled host;
As at the goal the paean they upraise,

He struck them with his forked lightning
    blaze.

(Str. 2)
To earthy from earth rebounding, down he
    crashed;
The fire-brand from his impious hand was
    dashed,
As like a Bacchic reveler on he came,
Outbreathing hate and flame,
And tottered. Elsewhere in the field,
Here, there, great Area like a war-horse
    wheeled;
Beneath his car down thrust
Our foemen bit the dust.

Seven captains at our seven gates
Thundered; for each a champion waits,
Each left behind his armor bright,
Trophy for Zeus who turns the fight;
Save two alone, that ill-starred pair
One mother to one father bare,
Who lance in rest, one 'gainst the other
Drave, and both perished, brother slain by
    brother.

(Ant. 2)
Now Victory to Thebes returns again

And smiles upon her chariot-circled plain.
Now let feast and festal should
Memories of war blot out.
Let us to the temples throng,
Dance and sing the live night long.
God of Thebes, lead thou the round.
Bacchus, shaker of the ground!
Let us end our revels here;
Lo! Creon our new lord draws near,
Crowned by this strange chance, our king.
What, I marvel, pondering?
Why this summons? Wherefore call
Us, his elders, one and all,
Bidding us with him debate,
On some grave concern of State?
[Enter CREON]

CREON
Elders, the gods have righted one again
Our storm-tossed ship of state, now safe in
    port.
But you by special summons I convened
As my most trusted councilors; first,
    because
I knew you loyal to Laius of old;
Again, when Oedipus restored our State,
Both while he ruled and when his rule was
    o'er,

Ye still were constant to the royal line.
Now that his two sons perished in one day,
Brother by brother murderously slain,
By right of kinship to the Princes dead,
I claim and hold the throne and sov-
    ereignty.
Yet 'tis no easy matter to discern
The temper of a man, his mind and will,
Till he be proved by exercise of power;
And in my case, if one who reigns
    supreme
Swerve from the highest policy,
    tongue-tied
By fear of consequence, that man I hold,
And ever held, the basest of the base.
And I contemn the man who sets his
    friend
Before his country. For myself, I call
To witness Zeus, whose eyes are
    everywhere,
If I perceive some mischievous design
To sap the State, I will not hold my
    tongue;
Nor would I reckon as my private friend
A public foe, well knowing that the State
Is the good ship that holds our fortunes all:
Farewell to friendship, if she suffers wreck.
Such is the policy by which I seek

To serve the Commons and conformably
I have proclaimed an edict as concerns
The sons of Oedipus; Eteocles
Who in his country's battle fought and fell,
The foremost champion—duly bury him
With all observances and ceremonies
That are the guerdon of the heroic dead.
But for the miscreant exile who returned
Minded in flames and ashes to blot out
His father's city and his father's gods,
And glut his vengeance with his kinsmen's
    blood,
Or drag them captive at his chariot
    wheels—
For Polyneices 'tis ordained that none
Shall give him burial or make mourn
    for him,
But leave his corpse unburied, to be meat
For dogs and carrion crows, a ghastly
    sight.
So am I purposed; never by my will
Shall miscreants take precedence of
    true men,
But all good patriots, alive or dead,
Shall be by me preferred and honored.

CHORUS
Son of Menoeceus, thus thou will'st
    to deal
With him who loathed and him who loved
    our State.
Thy word is law; thou canst dispose of us
The living, as thou will'st, as of the dead.

CREON
See then ye execute what I ordain.

CHORUS
On younger shoulders lay this grievous
    charge.

CREON
Fear not, I've posted guards to watch the
    corpse.

CHORUS
What further duty would'st thou lay on us?

CREON
Not to connive at disobedience.

CHORUS
No man is mad enough to court his death.

CREON

The penalty is death: yet hope of gain
Hath lured men to their ruin oftentimes.
[Enter GUARD]

GUARD

My lord, I will not make pretense to pant
And puff as some light-footed messenger.
In sooth my soul beneath its pack of
    thought
Made many a halt and turned and turned
    again;
For conscience plied her spur and curb by
    turns.
"Why hurry headlong to thy fate, poor
    fool?"
She whispered. Then again, "If Creon
    learn
This from another, thou wilt rue it worse."
Thus leisurely I hastened on my road;
Much thought extends a furlong to a
    league.
But in the end the forward voice
    prevailed,
To face thee. I will speak though I say
    nothing.
For plucking courage from despair
    methought,

'Let the worst hap, thou canst but meet thy
    fate.'

CREON
What is thy news? Why this despondency?

GUARD
Let me premise a word about myself?
I neither did the deed nor saw it done,
Nor were it just that I should come to
    harm.

CREON
Thou art good at parry, and canst fence
    about
Some matter of grave import, as is plain.

GUARD
The bearer of dread tidings needs must
    quake.

CREON
Then, sirrah, shoot thy bolt and get thee
    gone.

GUARD
Well, it must out; the corpse is buried;
    someone

E'en now besprinkled it with thirsty dust,
Performed the proper ritual—and was
    gone.

CREON
What say'st thou? Who hath dared to do
    this thing?

GUARD
I cannot tell, for there was ne'er a trace
Of pick or mattock—hard unbroken
    ground,
Without a scratch or rut of chariot
    wheels,
No sign that human hands had been at
    work.
When the first sentry of the morning
    watch
Gave the alarm, we all were terror-
    stricken.
The corpse had vanished, not interred in
    earth,
But strewn with dust, as if by one who
    sought
To avert the curse that haunts the un-
    buried dead:
Of hound or ravening jackal, not a sign.
Thereat arose an angry war of words;

Guard railed at guard and blows were like
    to end it,
For none was there to part us, each in turn
Suspected, but the guilt brought home to
    none,
From lack of evidence. We challenged
    each
The ordeal, or to handle red-hot iron,
Or pass through fire, affirming on
    our oath
Our innocence—we neither did the deed
Ourselves, nor know who did or com-
    passed it.
Our quest was at a standstill, when one
    spake
And bowed us all to earth like quivering
    reeds,
For there was no gainsaying him nor way
To escape perdition: Yeareboundtotell
TheKing,yecannothideit; so he spake.
And he convinced us all; so lots were cast,
And I, unlucky scapegoat, drew the prize.
So here I am unwilling and withal
Unwelcome; no man cares to hear ill
    news.

CHORUS
I had misgivings from the first, my liege,

Of something more than natural at work.

CREON

O cease, you vex me with your bab-
     blement;
I am like to think you dote in your old age.
Is it not arrant folly to pretend
That gods would have a thought for this
     dead man?
Did they forsooth award him special grace,
And as some benefactor bury him,
Who came to fire their hallowed sanc-
     tuaries,
To sack their shrines, to desolate their
     land,
And scout their ordinances? Or perchance
The gods bestow their favors on the bad.
No! no! I have long noted malcontents
Who wagged their heads, and kicked
     against the yoke,
Misliking these my orders, and my rule.
'Tis they, I warrant, who suborned my
     guards
By bribes. Of evils current upon earth
The worst is money. Money 'tis that sacks
Cities, and drives men forth from hearth
     and home;
Warps and seduces native innocence,

And breeds a habit of dishonesty.
But they who sold themselves shall find
    their greed
Out-shot the mark, and rue it soon or late.
Yea, as I still revere the dread of Zeus,
By Zeus I swear, except ye find and bring
Before my presence here the very man
Who carried out this lawless burial,
Death for your punishment shall not
    suffice.
Hanged on a cross, alive ye first shall make
Confession of this outrage. This will
    teach you
What practices are like to serve your turn.
There are some villainies that bring no
    gain.
For by dishonesty the few may thrive,
The many come to ruin and disgrace.

GUARD
May I not speak, or must I turn and go
Without a word?—

CREON
Begone! canst thou not see
That e'en this question irks me?

GUARD
Where, my lord?
Is it thy ears that suffer, or thy heart?

CREON
Why seek to probe and find the seat of
    pain?

GUARD
I gall thine ears—this miscreant thy mind.

CREON
What an inveterate babbler! get thee gone!

GUARD
Babbler perchance, but innocent of the
    crime.

CREON
Twice guilty, having sold thy soul for gain.

GUARD
Alas! how sad when reasoners reason
    wrong.

CREON
Go, quibble with thy reason. If thou fail'st
To find these malefactors, thou shalt own

The wages of ill-gotten gains is death.
[Exit CREON]

GUARD
I pray he may be found. But caught or not
(And fortune must determine that) thou
    never
Shalt see me here returning; that is sure.
For past all hope or thought I have
    escaped,
And for my safety owe the gods much
    thanks.

CHORUS
(Str. 1)
Many wonders there be, but naught more
    wondrous than man;
Over the surging sea, with a whitening
    south wind wan,
Through the foam of the firth, man makes
    his perilous way;
And the eldest of deities Earth that knows
    not toil nor decay
Ever he furrows and scores, as his team,
    year in year out,
With breed of the yoked horse, the
    ploughshare turneth about.

(Ant. 1)

The light-witted birds of the air, the beasts
    of the weald and the wood
He traps with his woven snare, and the
    brood of the briny flood.
Master of cunning he: the savage bull, and
    the hart
Who roams the mountain free, are tamed
    by his infinite art;
And the shaggy rough-maned steed is
    broken to bear the bit.

(Str. 2)

Speech and the wind-swift speed of
    counsel and civic wit,
He hath learnt for himself all these; and
    the arrowy rain to fly
And the nipping airs that freeze, 'neath the
    open winter sky.
He hath provision for all: fell plague he
    hath learnt to endure;
Safe whate'er may befall: yet for death he
    hath found no cure.

(Ant. 2)

Passing the wildest flight thought are the
    cunning and skill,
That guide man now to the light, but now

to counsels of ill.
If he honors the laws of the land, and
    reveres the Gods of the State
Proudly his city shall stand; but a cityless
    outcast I rate
Whoso bold in his pride from the path of
    right doth depart;
Ne'er may I sit by his side, or share the
    thoughts of his heart.

What strange vision meets my eyes,
Fills me with a wild surprise?
Sure I know her, sure 'tis she,
The maid Antigone.
Hapless child of hapless sire,
Didst thou recklessly conspire,
Madly brave the King's decree?
Therefore are they haling thee?
[Enter GUARD bringing ANTIGONE]

GUARD
Here is the culprit taken in the act
Of giving burial. But where's the King?

CHORUS
There from the palace he returns in time.
[Enter CREON]

CREON

Why is my presence timely? What has
    chanced?

GUARD

No man, my lord, should make a vow,
    for if
He ever swears he will not do a thing,
His afterthoughts belie his first resolve.
When from the hail-storm of thy threats
    I fled
I sware thou wouldst not see me here
    again;
But the wild rapture of a glad surprise
Intoxicates, and so I'm here forsworn.
And here's my prisoner, caught in the
    very act,
Decking the grave. No lottery this time;
This prize is mine by right of treasure-
    trove.
So take her, judge her, rack her, if thou
    wilt.
She's thine, my liege; but I may rightly
    claim
Hence to depart well quit of all these ills.

CREON

Say, how didst thou arrest the maid, and
    where?

GUARD

Burying the man. There's nothing more to
    tell.

CREON

Hast thou thy wits? Or know'st thou what
    thou say'st?

GUARD

I saw this woman burying the corpse
Against thy orders. Is that clear and plain?

CREON

But how was she surprised and caught in
    the act?

GUARD

It happened thus. No sooner had we
    come,
Driven from thy presence by those awful
    threats,
Than straight we swept away all trace of
    dust,
And bared the clammy body. Then we sat

High on the ridge to windward of the
    stench,
While each man kept he fellow alert and
    rated
Roundly the sluggard if he chanced
    to nap.
So all night long we watched, until the sun
Stood high in heaven, and his blazing
    beams
Smote us. A sudden whirlwind then
    upraised
A cloud of dust that blotted out the sky,
And swept the plain, and stripped the
    woodlands bare,
And shook the firmament. We closed
    our eyes
And waited till the heaven-sent plague
    should pass.
At last it ceased, and lo! there stood this
    maid.
A piercing cry she uttered, sad and shrill,
As when the mother bird beholds her nest
Robbed of its nestlings; even so the maid
Wailed as she saw the body stripped and
    bare,
And cursed the ruffians who had done this
    deed.
Anon she gathered handfuls of dry dust,

Then, holding high a well-wrought
    brazen urn,
Thrice on the dead she poured a lustral
    stream.
We at the sight swooped down on her and
    seized
Our quarry. Undismayed she stood,
    and when
We taxed her with the former crime and
    this,
She disowned nothing. I was glad—and
    grieved;
For 'tis most sweet to 'scape oneself scot-
    free,
And yet to bring disaster to a friend
Is grievous. Take it all in all, I deem
A man's first duty is to serve himself.

CREON
Speak, girl, with head bent low and down-
    cast eyes,
Does thou plead guilty or deny the deed?

ANTIGONE
Guilty. I did it, I deny it not.

CREON (to GUARD)
Sirrah, begone whither thou wilt, and
    thank
Thy luck that thou hast 'scaped a heavy
    charge.
(To ANTIGONE)
Now answer this plain question, yes or no,
Wast thou acquainted with the interdict?

ANTIGONE
I knew, all knew; how should I fail to
    know?

CREON
And yet wert bold enough to break
    the law?

ANTIGONE
Yea, for these laws were not ordained of
    Zeus,
And she who sits enthroned with gods
    below,
Justice, enacted not these human laws.
Nor did I deem that thou, a mortal man,
Could'st by a breath annul and override
The immutable unwritten laws of
    Heaven.
They were not born today nor yesterday;

They die not; and none knoweth whence
    they sprang.
I was not like, who feared no mortal's
    frown,
To disobey these laws and so provoke
The wrath of Heaven. I knew that I
    must die,
E'en hadst thou not proclaimed it; and if
    death
Is thereby hastened, I shall count it gain.
For death is gain to him whose life, like
    mine,
Is full of misery. Thus my lot appears
Not sad, but blissful; for had I endured
To leave my mother's son unburied there,
I should have grieved with reason, but
    not now.
And if in this thou judgest me a fool,
Methinks the judge of folly's not acquit.

CHORUS
A stubborn daughter of a stubborn sire,
This ill-starred maiden kicks against the
    pricks.

CREON
Well, let her know the stubbornest of wills
Are soonest bended, as the hardest iron,

O'er-heated in the fire to brittleness,
Flies soonest into fragments, shivered
    through.
A snaffle curbs the fieriest steed, and he
Who in subjection lives must needs be
    meek.
But this proud girl, in insolence well-
    schooled,
First overstepped the established law, and
    then—
A second and worse act of insolence—
She boasts and glories in her wickedness.
Now if she thus can flout authority
Unpunished, I am woman, she the man.
But though she be my sister's child or
    nearer
Of kin than all who worship at my hearth,
Nor she nor yet her sister shall escape
The utmost penalty, for both I hold,
As arch-conspirators, of equal guilt.
Bring forth the older; even now I saw her
Within the palace, frenzied and distraught.
The workings of the mind discover oft
Dark deeds in darkness schemed, before
    the act.
More hateful still the miscreant who seeks
When caught, to make a virtue of a crime.

ANTIGONE

Would'st thou do more than slay thy
    prisoner?

CREON

Not I, thy life is mine, and that's enough.

ANTIGONE

Why dally then? To me no word of thine
Is pleasant: God forbid it e'er should
    please;
Nor am I more acceptable to thee.
And yet how otherwise had I achieved
A name so glorious as by burying
A brother? so my townsmen all would say,
Where they not gagged by terror, Manifold
A king's prerogatives, and not the least
That all his acts and all his words are law.

CREON

Of all these Thebans none so deems but
    thou.

ANTIGONE

These think as I, but bate their breath to
    thee.

CREON

Hast thou no shame to differ from all
these?

ANTIGONE

To reverence kith and kin can bring no
shame.

CREON

Was his dead foeman not thy kinsman too?

ANTIGONE

One mother bare them and the self-same
sire.

CREON

Why cast a slur on one by honoring one?

ANTIGONE

The dead man will not bear thee out in
this.

CREON

Surely, if good and evil fare alive.

ANTIGONE

The slain man was no villain but a
brother.

CREON
The patriot perished by the outlaw's
    brand.

ANTIGONE
Nathless the realms below these rites
    require.

CREON
Not that the base should fare as do the
    brave.

ANTIGONE
Who knows if this world's crimes are
    virtues there?

CREON
Not even death can make a foe a friend.

ANTIGONE
My nature is for mutual love, not hate.

CREON
Die then, and love the dead if thou must;
No woman shall be the master while I live.
[Enter ISMENE]

CHORUS

Lo from out the palace gate,
Weeping o'er her sister's fate,
Comes Ismene; see her brow,
Once serene, beclouded now,
See her beauteous face o'erspread
With a flush of angry red.

CREON

Woman, who like a viper unperceived
Didst harbor in my house and drain my
    blood,
Two plagues I nurtured blindly, so it
    proved,
To sap my throne. Say, didst thou too abet
This crime, or dost abjure all privity?

ISMENE

I did the deed, if she will have it so,
And with my sister claim to share the guilt.

ANTIGONE

That were unjust. Thou would'st not act
    with me
At first, and I refused thy partnership.

ISMENE

But now thy bark is stranded, I am bold

To claim my share as partner in the loss.

ANTIGONE
Who did the deed the under-world knows
    well:
A friend in word is never friend of mine.

ISMENE
O sister, scorn me not, let me but share
Thy work of piety, and with thee die.

ANTIGONE
Claim not a work in which thou hadst no
    hand;
One death sufficeth. Wherefore should'st
    thou die?

ISMENE
What would life profit me bereft of thee?

ANTIGONE
Ask Creon, he's thy kinsman and best
    friend.

ISMENE
Why taunt me? Find'st thou pleasure in
    these gibes?

ANTIGONE
'Tis a sad mockery, if indeed I mock.

ISMENE
O say if I can help thee even now.

ANTIGONE
No, save thyself; I grudge not thy escape.

ISMENE
Is e'en this boon denied, to share thy lot?

ANTIGONE
Yea, for thou chosed'st life, and I to die.

ISMENE
Thou canst not say that I did not protest.

ANTIGONE
Well, some approved thy wisdom, others
    mine.

ISMENE
But now we stand convicted, both alike.

ANTIGONE
Fear not; thou livest, I died long ago
Then when I gave my life to save the dead.

CREON

Both maids, methinks, are crazed. One
    suddenly
Has lost her wits, the other was born mad.

ISMENE

Yea, so it falls, sire, when misfortune
    comes,
The wisest even lose their mother wit.

CREON

I' faith thy wit forsook thee when thou
    mad'st
Thy choice with evil-doers to do ill.

ISMENE

What life for me without my sister here?

CREON

Say not thy sister here: thy sister's dead.

ISMENE

What, wilt thou slay thy own son's plighted
    bride?

CREON

Aye, let him raise him seed from other
    fields.

ISMENE
No new espousal can be like the old.

CREON
A plague on trulls who court and woo our
    sons.

ANTIGONE
O Haemon, how thy sire dishonors thee!

CREON
A plague on thee and thy accursed bride!

CHORUS
What, wilt thou rob thine own son of his
    bride?

CREON
'Tis death that bars this marriage, not his
    sire.

CHORUS
So her death-warrant, it would seem, is
    sealed.

CREON
By you, as first by me; off with them,
    guards,

And keep them close. Henceforward let
   them learn
To live as women use, not roam at large.
For e'en the bravest spirits run away
When they perceive death pressing on life's
   heels.

CHORUS
(Str. 1)
Thrice blest are they who never tasted
   pain!
If once the curse of Heaven attaint a race,
The infection lingers on and speeds apace,
Age after age, and each the cup must
   drain.

So when Etesian blasts from Thrace
   downpour
Sweep o'er the blackening main and whirl
   to land
From Ocean's cavernous depths his ooze
   and sand,
Billow on billow thunders on the shore.

(Ant. 1)
On the Labdacidae I see descending
Woe upon woe; from days of old some god
Laid on the race a malison, and his rod

Scourges each age with sorrows never
    ending.

The light that dawned upon its last
    born son
Is vanished, and the bloody axe of Fate
Has felled the goodly tree that blossomed
    late.
O Oedipus, by reckless pride undone!

(Str. 2)
Thy might, O Zeus, what mortal power
    can quell?
Not sleep that lays all else beneath its spell,
Nor moons that never tire: untouched by
    Time,
Throned in the dazzling light
That crowns Olympus' height,
Thou reignest King, omnipotent, sublime.
Past, present, and to be,
All bow to thy decree,
All that exceeds the mean by Fate
Is punished, Love or Hate.

(Ant. 2)
Hope flits about never-wearying wings;
Profit to some, to some light loves she
    brings,

But no man knoweth how her gifts may
     turn,
Till 'neath his feet the treacherous ashes
     burn.
Sure 'twas a sage inspired that spake this
     word;
If evil good appear
To any, Fate is near;
And brief the respite from her flaming
     sword.
Hither comes in angry mood
Haemon, latest of thy brood;
Is it for his bride he's grieved,
Or her marriage-bed deceived,
Doth he make his mourn for thee,
Maid forlorn, Antigone?
[Enter HAEMON]

CREON
Soon shall we know, better than seer can
     tell.
Learning may fixed decree anent thy
     bride,
Thou mean'st not, son, to rave against thy
     sire?
Know'st not whate'er we do is done in
     love?

HAEMON

O father, I am thine, and I will take
Thy wisdom as the helm to steer withal.
Therefore no wedlock shall by me be held
More precious than thy loving goverance.

CREON

Well spoken: so right-minded sons should
        feel,
In all deferring to a father's will.
For 'tis the hope of parents they may rear
A brood of sons submissive, keen to
        avenge
Their father's wrongs, and count his
        friends their own.
But who begets unprofitable sons,
He verily breeds trouble for himself,
And for his foes much laughter. Son, be
        warned
And let no woman fool away thy wits.
Ill fares the husband mated with a shrew,
And her embraces very soon wax cold.
For what can wound so surely to the quick
As a false friend? So spue and cast her off,
Bid her go find a husband with the dead.
For since I caught her openly rebelling,
Of all my subjects the one malcontent,
I will not prove a traitor to the State.

She surely dies. Go, let her, if she will,
Appeal to Zeus the God of Kindred, for
If thus I nurse rebellion in my house,
Shall not I foster mutiny without?
For whoso rules his household worthily,
Will prove in civic matters no less wise.
But he who overbears the laws, or thinks
To overrule his rulers, such as one
I never will allow. Whome'er the State
Appoints must be obeyed in everything,
But small and great, just and unjust alike.
I warrant such a one in either case
Would shine, as King or subject; such
    a man
Would in the storm of battle stand his
    ground,
A comrade leal and true; but Anarchy—
What evils are not wrought by Anarchy!
She ruins States, and overthrows the
    home,
She dissipates and routs the embattled
    host;
While discipline preserves the ordered
    ranks.
Therefore we must maintain authority
And yield to title to a woman's will.
Better, if needs be, men should cast
    us out

Than hear it said, a woman proved his
    match.

CHORUS
To me, unless old age have dulled wits,
Thy words appear both reasonable and
    wise.

HAEMON
Father, the gods implant in mortal men
Reason, the choicest gift bestowed by
    heaven.
'Tis not for me to say thou errest, nor
Would I arraign thy wisdom, if I could;
And yet wise thoughts may come to
    other men
And, as thy son, it falls to me to mark
The acts, the words, the comments of the
    crowd.
The commons stand in terror of thy
    frown,
And dare not utter aught that might
    offend,
But I can overhear their muttered plaints,
Know how the people mourn this maiden
    doomed
For noblest deeds to die the worst of
    deaths.

When her own brother slain in battle lay
Unsepulchered, she suffered not his corse
To lie for carrion birds and dogs to maul:
Should not her name (they cry) be writ in
    gold?
Such the low murmurings that reach
    my ear.
O father, nothing is by me more prized
Than thy well-being, for what higher good
Can children covet than their sire's fair
    fame,
As fathers too take pride in glorious sons?
Therefore, my father, cling not to one
    mood,
And deemed not thou art right, all others
    wrong.
For whoso thinks that wisdom dwells
    with him,
That he alone can speak or think aright,
Such oracles are empty breath when tried.
The wisest man will let himself be swayed
By others' wisdom and relax in time.
See how the trees beside a stream in flood
Save, if they yield to force, each spray
    unharmed,
But by resisting perish root and branch.
The mariner who keeps his mainsheet
    taut,

And will not slacken in the gale, is like
To sail with thwarts reversed, keel up-
    permost.
Relent then and repent thee of thy wrath;
For, if one young in years may claim some
    sense,
I'll say 'tis best of all to be endowed
With absolute wisdom; but, if that's
    denied,
(And nature takes not readily that ply)
Next wise is he who lists to sage advice.

CHORUS
If he says aught in season, heed him,
    King.
(To HAEMON)
Heed thou thy sire too; both have spoken
    well.

CREON
What, would you have us at our age be
    schooled,
Lessoned in prudence by a beardless boy?

HAEMON
I plead for justice, father, nothing more.
Weigh me upon my merit, not my years.

CREON
Strange merit this to sanction lawlessness!

HAEMON
For evil-doers I would urge no plea.

CREON
Is not this maid an arrant law-breaker?

HAEMON
The Theban commons with one voice
    say, No.

CREON
What, shall the mob dictate my policy?

HAEMON
'Tis thou, methinks, who speakest like
    a boy.

CREON
Am I to rule for others, or myself?

HAEMON
A State for one man is no State at all.

CREON
The State is his who rules it, so 'tis held.

HAEMON

As monarch of a desert thou wouldst
    shine.

CREON

This boy, methinks, maintains the woman's
    cause.

HAEMON

If thou be'st woman, yes. My thought's for
    thee.

CREON

O reprobate, would'st wrangle with thy
    sire?

HAEMON

Because I see thee wrongfully perverse.

CREON

And am I wrong, if I maintain my rights?

HAEMON

Talk not of rights; thou spurn'st the due of
    Heaven

CREON

O heart corrupt, a woman's minion thou!

HAEMON
Slave to dishonor thou wilt never find me.

CREON
Thy speech at least was all a plea for her.

HAEMON
And thee and me, and for the gods below.

CREON
Living the maid shall never be thy bride.

HAEMON
So she shall die, but one will die with her.

CREON
Hast come to such a pass as threaten me?

HAEMON
What threat is this, vain counsels to
    reprove?

CREON
Vain fool to instruct thy betters; thou shall
    rue it.

HAEMON
Wert not my father, I had said thou err'st.

CREON
Play not the spaniel, thou a woman's slave.

HAEMON
When thou dost speak, must no man make
    reply?

CREON
This passes bounds. By heaven, thou shalt
    not rate
And jeer and flout me with impunity.
Off with the hateful thing that she may die
At once, beside her bridegroom, in his
    sight.

HAEMON
Think not that in my sight the maid
    shall die,
Or by my side; never shalt thou again
Behold my face hereafter. Go, consort
With friends who like a madman for their
    mate.
[Exit HAEMON]

CHORUS
Thy son has gone, my liege, in angry
    haste.
Fell is the wrath of youth beneath a smart.

CREON

Let him go vent his fury like a fiend:
These sisters twain he shall not save from
    death.

CHORUS

Surely, thou meanest not to slay them
    both?

CREON

I stand corrected; only her who touched
The body.

CHORUS

And what death is she to die?

CREON

She shall be taken to some desert place
By man untrod, and in a rock-hewn cave,
With food no more than to avoid the taint
That homicide might bring on all the
    State,
Buried alive. There let her call in aid
The King of Death, the one god she
    reveres,
Or learn too late a lesson learnt at last:
'Tis labor lost, to reverence the dead.

CHORUS

(Str.)

Love resistless in fight, all yield at a glance
    of thine eye,
Love who pillowed all night on a maiden's
    cheek dost lie,
Over the upland holds. Shall mortals not
    yield to thee?

(Ant).

Mad are thy subjects all, and even the
    wisest heart
Straight to folly will fall, at a touch of thy
    poisoned dart.
Thou didst kindle the strife, this feud of
    kinsman with kin,
By the eyes of a winsome wife, and the
    yearning her heart to win.
For as her consort still, enthroned with Jus-
    tice above,
Thou bendest man to thy will, O all invin-
    cible Love.

Lo I myself am borne aside,
From Justice, as I view this bride.
(O sight an eye in tears to drown)
Antigone, so young, so fair,
Thus hurried down

Death's bower with the dead to share.

ANTIGONE
(Str. 1)
Friends, countrymen, my last farewell I
    make;
My journey's done.
One last fond, lingering, longing look
    I take
At the bright sun.
For Death who puts to sleep both young
    and old
Hales my young life,
And beckons me to Acheron's dark fold,
An unwed wife.
No youths have sung the marriage song
    for me,
My bridal bed
No maids have strewn with flowers from
    the lea,
'Tis Death I wed.

CHORUS
But bethink thee, thou art sped,
Great and glorious, to the dead.
Thou the sword's edge hast not tasted,
No disease thy frame hath wasted.
Freely thou alone shalt go

Living to the dead below.

ANTIGONE
(Ant. 1)
Nay, but the piteous tale I've heard
    men tell
Of Tantalus' doomed child,
Chained upon Siphylus' high rocky fell,
That clung like ivy wild,
Drenched by the pelting rain and whirling
    snow,
Left there to pine,
While on her frozen breast the tears aye
    flow—
Her fate is mine.

CHORUS
She was sprung of gods, divine,
Mortals we of mortal line.
Like renown with gods to gain
Recompenses all thy pain.
Take this solace to thy tomb
Hers in life and death thy doom.

ANTIGONE
(Str. 2)
Alack, alack! Ye mock me. Is it meet
Thus to insult me living, to my face?

Cease, by our country's altars I entreat,
Ye lordly rulers of a lordly race.
O fount of Dirce, wood-embowered plain
Where Theban chariots to victory speed,
Mark ye the cruel laws that now have
      wrought my bane,
The friends who show no pity in my need!
Was ever fate like mine? O monstrous
      doom,
Within a rock-built prison sepulchered,
To fade and wither in a living tomb,
And alien midst the living and the dead.

CHORUS
(Str. 3)
In thy boldness over-rash
Madly thou thy foot didst dash
'Gainst high Justice' altar stair.
Thou a father's guild dost bear.

ANTIGONE
(Ant. 2)
At this thou touchest my most poignant
      pain,
My ill-starred father's piteous disgrace,
The taint of blood, the hereditary stain,
That clings to all of Labdacus' famed
      race.

Woe worth the monstrous marriage-bed
    where lay
A mother with the son her womb had
    borne,
Therein I was conceived, woe worth
    the day,
Fruit of incestuous sheets, a maid forlorn,
And now I pass, accursed and unwed,
To meet them as an alien there below;
And thee, O brother, in marriage ill-
    bestead,
'Twas thy dead hand that dealt me this
    death-blow.

CHORUS
Religion has her chains, 'tis true,
Let rite be paid when rites are due.
Yet is it ill to disobey
The powers who hold by might the sway.
Thou hast withstood authority,
A self-willed rebel, thou must die.

ANTIGONE
Unwept, unwed, unfriended, hence I go,
No longer may I see the day's bright eye;
Not one friend left to share my bitter woe,
And o'er my ashes heave one passing sigh.

CREON

If wail and lamentation aught availed
To stave off death, I trow they'd
    never end.
Away with her, and having walled her up
In a rock-vaulted tomb, as I ordained,
Leave her alone at liberty to die,
Or, if she choose, to live in solitude,
The tomb her dwelling. We in either case
Are guiltless as concerns this maiden's
    blood,
Only on earth no lodging shall she find.

ANTIGONE

O grave, O bridal bower, O prison house
Hewn from the rock, my everlasting home,
Whither I go to join the mighty host
Of kinsfolk, Persephassa's guests long
    dead,
The last of all, of all more miserable,
I pass, my destined span of years cut short.
And yet good hope is mine that I shall find
A welcome from my sire, a welcome too,
From thee, my mother, and my brother
    dear;
From with these hands, I laved and decked
    your limbs

In death, and poured libations on your
    grave.
And last, my Polyneices, unto thee
I paid due rites, and this my recompense!
Yet am I justified in wisdom's eyes.
For even had it been some child of mine,
Or husband mouldering in death's decay,
I had not wrought this deed despite the
    State.
What is the law I call in aid? 'Tis thus
I argue. Had it been a husband dead
I might have wed another, and have borne
Another child, to take the dead child's
    place.
But, now my sire and mother both are
    dead,
No second brother can be born for me.
Thus by the law of conscience I was led
To honor thee, dear brother, and was
    judged
By Creon guilty of a heinous crime.
And now he drags me like a criminal,
A bride unwed, amerced of marriage-song
And marriage-bed and joys of
    motherhood,
By friends deserted to a living grave.
What ordinance of heaven have I trans-
    gressed?

Hereafter can I look to any god
For succor, call on any man for help?
Alas, my piety is impious deemed.
Well, if such justice is approved of heaven,
I shall be taught by suffering my sin;
But if the sin is theirs, O may they suffer
No worse ills than the wrongs they do
    to me.

CHORUS
The same ungovernable will
Drives like a gale the maiden still.

CREON
Therefore, my guards who let her stay
Shall smart full sore for their delay.

ANTIGONE
Ah, woe is me! This word I hear
Brings death most near.

CHORUS
I have no comfort. What he saith,
Portends no other thing than death.

ANTIGONE
My fatherland, city of Thebes divine,
Ye gods of Thebes whence sprang my line,

Look, puissant lords of Thebes, on me;
The last of all your royal house ye see.
Martyred by men of sin, undone.
Such meed my piety hath won.
[Exit ANTIGONE]

CHORUS
(Str. 1)
Like to thee that maiden bright,
Danae, in her brass-bound tower,
Once exchanged the glad sunlight
For a cell, her bridal bower.
And yet she sprang of royal line,
My child, like thine,
And nursed the seed
By her conceived
Of Zeus descending in a golden shower.
Strange are the ways of Fate, her power
Nor wealth, nor arms withstand, nor
        tower;
Nor brass-prowed ships, that breast the sea
From Fate can flee.

(Ant. 1)
Thus Dryas' child, the rash Edonian King,
For words of high disdain
Did Bacchus to a rocky dungeon bring,
To cool the madness of a fevered brain.

His frenzy passed,
He learnt at last
'Twas madness gibes against a god to fling.
For once he fain had quenched the Mae-
    nad's fire;
And of the tuneful Nine provoked the ire.

(Str. 2)
By the Iron Rocks that guard the double
    main,
On Bosporus' lone strand,
Where stretcheth Salmydessus' plain
In the wild Thracian land,
There on his borders Ares witnessed
The vengeance by a jealous step-dame
    ta'en
The gore that trickled from a spindle red,
The sightless orbits of her step-sons twain.

(Ant. 2)
Wasting away they mourned their piteous
    doom,
The blasted issue of their mother's womb.
But she her lineage could trace
To great Erechtheus' race;
Daughter of Boreas in her sire's vast caves
Reared, where the tempest raves,
Swift as his horses o'er the hills she sped;

A child of gods; yet she, my child, like
    thee,
By Destiny
That knows not death nor age—she too
    was vanquished.
[Enter TEIRESIAS and BOY]

TEIRESIAS
Princes of Thebes, two wayfarers as one,
Having betwixt us eyes for one, we are
    here.
The blind man cannot move without a
    guide.

CREON
Why tidings, old Teiresias?

TEIRESIAS
I will tell thee;
And when thou hearest thou must heed
    the seer.

CREON
Thus far I ne'er have disobeyed thy rede.

TEIRESIAS
So hast thou steered the ship of State
    aright.

CREON
I know it, and I gladly own my debt.

TEIRESIAS
Bethink thee that thou treadest once again
The razor edge of peril.

CREON
What is this?
Thy words inspire a dread presentiment.

TEIRESIAS
The divination of my arts shall tell.
Sitting upon my throne of augury,
As is my wont, where every fowl of heaven
Find harborage, upon mine ears was
    borne
A jargon strange of twitterings, hoots, and
    screams;
So knew I that each bird at the other tare
With bloody talons, for the whirr of wings
Could signify naught else. Perturbed in
    soul,
I straight essayed the sacrifice by fire
On blazing altars, but the God of Fire
Came not in flame, and from the thigh
    bones dripped
And sputtered in the ashes a foul ooze;

Gall-bladders cracked and spurted up:
    the fat
Melted and fell and left the thigh bones
    bare.
Such are the signs, taught by this lad, I
    read—
As I guide others, so the boy guides me—
The frustrate signs of oracles grown
    dumb.
O King, thy willful temper ails the State,
For all our shrines and altars are profaned
By what has filled the maw of dogs and
    crows,
The flesh of Oedipus' unburied son.
Therefore the angry gods abominate
Our litanies and our burnt offerings;
Therefore no birds trill out a happy note,
Gorged with the carnival of human gore.
O ponder this, my son. To err is common
To all men, but the man who having erred
Hugs not his errors, but repents and seeks
The cure, is not a wastrel nor unwise.
No fool, the saw goes, like the obstinate
    fool.
Let death disarm thy vengeance. O
    forbear
To vex the dead. What glory wilt
    thou win

By slaying twice the slain? I mean thee
    well;
Counsel's most welcome if I promise gain.

CREON
Old man, ye all let fly at me your shafts
Like anchors at a target; yea, ye set
Your soothsayer on me. Peddlers are ye all
And I the merchandise ye buy and sell.
Go to, and make your profit where ye will,
Silver of Sardis change for gold of Ind;
Ye will not purchase this man's burial,
Not though the winged ministers of Zeus
Should bear him in their talons to his
    throne;
Not e'en in awe of prodigy so dire
Would I permit his burial, for I know
No human soilure can assail the gods;
This too I know, Teiresias, dire's the fall
Of craft and cunning when it tries to gloss
Foul treachery with fair words for filthy
    gain.

TEIRESIAS
Alas! doth any know and lay to heart—

CREON
Is this the prelude to some hackneyed saw?

TEIRESIAS
How far good counsel is the best of goods?

CREON
True, as unwisdom is the worst of ills.

TEIRESIAS
Thou art infected with that ill thyself.

CREON
I will not bandy insults with thee, seer.

TEIRESIAS
And yet thou say'st my prophesies are
     frauds.

CREON
Prophets are all a money-getting tribe.

TEIRESIAS
And kings are all a lucre-loving race.

CREON
Dost know at whom thou glancest, me thy
     lord?

TEIRESIAS
Lord of the State and savior, thanks to me.

CREON
Skilled prophet art thou, but to wrong
    inclined.

TEIRESIAS
Take heed, thou wilt provoke me to reveal
The mystery deep hidden in my breast.

CREON
Say on, but see it be not said for gain.

TEIRESIAS
Such thou, methinks, till now hast judged
    my words.

CREON
Be sure thou wilt not traffic on my wits.

TEIRESIAS
Know then for sure, the coursers of
    the sun
Not many times shall run their race, before
Thou shalt have given the fruit of thine
    own loins
In quittance of thy murder, life for life;
For that thou hast entombed a living
    soul,
And sent below a denizen of earth,

And wronged the nether gods by leaving
    here
A corpse unlaved, unwept, unsepulchered.
Herein thou hast no part, nor e'en
    the gods
In heaven; and thou usurp'st a power not
    thine.
For this the avenging spirits of Heaven
    and Hell
Who dog the steps of sin are on thy trail:
What these have suffered thou shalt
    suffer too.
And now, consider whether bought by gold
I prophesy. For, yet a little while,
And sound of lamentation shall be heard,
Of men and women through thy desolate
    halls;
And all thy neighbor States are leagues to
    avenge
Their mangled warriors who have found a
    grave
I' the maw of wolf or hound, or
    winged bird
That flying homewards taints their
    city's air.
These are the shafts, that like a
    bowman I
Provoked to anger, loosen at thy breast,

Unerring, and their smart thou shalt not
    shun.
Boy, lead me home, that he may vent his
    spleen
On younger men, and learn to curb his
    tongue
With gentler manners than his present
    mood.
[Exit TEIRESIAS]

CHORUS
My liege, that man hath gone, foretelling
    woe.
And, O believe me, since these grizzled
    locks
Were like the raven, never have I known
The prophet's warning to the State to fail.

CREON
I know it too, and it perplexes me.
To yield is grievous, but the obstinate soul
That fights with Fate, is smitten grievously.

CHORUS
Son of Menoeceus, list to good advice.

CHORUS
What should I do. Advise me. I will heed.

CHORUS

Go, free the maiden from her rocky cell;
And for the unburied outlaw build a tomb.

CREON

Is that your counsel? You would have me
　　yield?

CHORUS

Yea, king, this instant. Vengeance of
　　the gods
Is swift to overtake the impenitent.

CREON

Ah! what a wrench it is to sacrifice
My heart's resolve; but Fate is ill to fight.

CHORUS

Go, trust not others. Do it quick thyself.

CREON

I go hot-foot. Bestir ye one and all,
My henchmen! Get ye axes! Speed away
To yonder eminence! I too will go,
For all my resolution this way sways.
'Twas I that bound, I too will set her
　　free.
Almost I am persuaded it is best

To keep through life the law ordained
    of old.
[Exit CREON]

CHORUS
(Str. 1)
Thou by many names adored,
Child of Zeus the God of thunder,
Of a Theban bride the wonder,
Fair Italia's guardian lord;

In the deep-embosomed glades
Of the Eleusinian Queen
Haunt of revelers, men and maids,
Dionysus, thou art seen.

Where Ismenus rolls his waters,
Where the Dragon's teeth were sown,
Where the Bacchanals thy daughters
Round thee roam,
There thy home;
Thebes, O Bacchus, is thine own.

(Ant. 1)
Thee on the two-crested rock
Lurid-flaming torches see;
Where Corisian maidens flock,
Thee the springs of Castaly.

By Nysa's bastion ivy-clad,
By shores with clustered vineyards glad,
There to thee the hymn rings out,
And through our streets we Thebans
    shout,
All hail to thee
Evoe, Evoe!

(Str. 2)
Oh, as thou lov'st this city best of all,
To thee, and to thy Mother levin-stricken,
In our dire need we call;
Thou see'st with what a plague our towns-
    folk sicken.
Thy ready help we crave,
Whether adown Parnassian heights de-
    scending,
Or o'er the roaring straits thy swift was
    wending,
Save us, O save!

(Ant. 2)
Brightest of all the orbs that breathe forth
    light,
Authentic son of Zeus, immortal king,
Leader of all the voices of the night,
Come, and thy train of Thyiads with thee
    bring,

Thy maddened rout
Who dance before thee all night long, and
    shout,
Thy handmaids we,
Evoe, Evoe!

[Enter MESSENGER]

MESSENGER
Attend all ye who dwell beside the halls
Of Cadmus and Amphion. No man's life
As of one tenor would I praise or blame,
For Fortune with a constant ebb and rise
Casts down and raises high and low alike,
And none can read a mortal's horoscope.
Take Creon; he, methought, if any man,
Was enviable. He had saved this land
Of Cadmus from our enemies and
    attained
A monarch's powers and ruled the state
    supreme,
While a right noble issue crowned his bliss.
Now all is gone and wasted, for a life
Without life's joys I count a living death.
You'll tell me he has ample store of
    wealth,
The pomp and circumstance of kings;
    but if

These give no pleasure, all the rest I count
The shadow of a shade, nor would I weigh
His wealth and power 'gainst a dram
    of joy.

CHORUS
What fresh woes bring'st thou to the royal
    house?

MESSENGER
Both dead, and they who live deserve
    to die.

CHORUS
Who is the slayer, who the victim? speak.

MESSENGER
Haemon; his blood shed by no stranger
    hand.

CHORUS
What mean ye? by his father's or his own?

MESSENGER
His own; in anger for his father's crime.

CHORUS

O prophet, what thou spakest comes to
    pass.

MESSENGER

So stands the case; now 'tis for you to act.

CHORUS

Lo! from the palace gates I see ap-
    proaching
Creon's unhappy wife, Eurydice.
Comes she by chance or learning her son's
    fate?
[Enter EURYDICE]

EURYDICE

Ye men of Thebes, I overheard your talk.
As I passed out to offer up my prayer
To Pallas, and was drawing back the bar
To open wide the door, upon my ears
There broke a wail that told of household
    woe
Stricken with terror in my handmaids'
    arms
I fell and fainted. But repeat your tale
To one not unacquaint with misery.

MESSENGER

Dear mistress, I was there and will relate
The perfect truth, omitting not one word.
Why should we gloze and flatter, to be
    proved
Liars hereafter? Truth is ever best.
Well, in attendance on my liege, your lord,
I crossed the plain to its utmost margin,
    where
The corse of Polyneices, gnawn and
    mauled,
Was lying yet. We offered first a prayer
To Pluto and the goddess of cross-ways,
With contrite hearts, to deprecate their ire.
Then laved with lustral waves the mangled
    corse,
Laid it on fresh-lopped branches, lit a
    pyre,
And to his memory piled a mighty mound
Of mother earth. Then to the caverned
    rock,
The bridal chamber of the maid and Death,
We sped, about to enter. But a guard
Heard from that godless shrine a far shrill
    wail,
And ran back to our lord to tell the news.
But as he nearer drew a hollow sound

Of lamentation to the King was borne.
He groaned and uttered then this bitter
    plaint:
"Am I a prophet? miserable me!
Is this the saddest path I ever trod?
'Tis my son's voice that calls me. On
    press on,
My henchmen, haste with double speed to
    the tomb
Where rocks down-torn have made a gap,
    look in
And tell me if in truth I recognize
The voice of Haemon or am heaven-
    deceived."
So at the bidding of our distraught lord
We looked, and in the craven's vaulted
    gloom
I saw the maiden lying strangled there,
A noose of linen twined about her neck;
And hard beside her, clasping her cold
    form,
Her lover lay bewailing his dead bride
Death-wedded, and his father's cruelty.
When the King saw him, with a terrible
    groan
He moved towards him, crying, "O
    my son

What hast thou done? What ailed thee?
    What mischance
Has reft thee of thy reason? O come forth,
Come forth, my son; thy father
    supplicates."
But the son glared at him with tiger eyes,
Spat in his face, and then, without a word,
Drew his two-hilted sword and smote, but
    missed
His father flying backwards. Then the boy,
Wroth with himself, poor wretch, in-
    continent
Fell on his sword and drove it through
    his side
Home, but yet breathing clasped in his
    lax arms
The maid, her pallid cheek incarnadined
With his expiring gasps. So there they lay
Two corpses, one in death. His marriage
    rites
Are consummated in the halls of Death:
A witness that of ills whate'er befall
Mortals' unwisdom is the worst of all.
[Exit EURYDICE]

CHORUS
What makest thou of this? The Queen
    has gone

Without a word importing good or ill.

MESSENGER

I marvel too, but entertain good hope.
'Tis that she shrinks in public to lament
Her son's sad ending, and in privacy
Would with her maidens mourn a private
    loss.
Trust me, she is discreet and will not err.

CHORUS

I know not, but strained silence, so I deem,
Is no less ominous than excessive grief.

MESSENGER

Well, let us to the house and solve our
    doubts,
Whether the tumult of her heart conceals
Some fell design. It may be thou art right:
Unnatural silence signifies no good.

CHORUS

Lo! the King himself appears.
Evidence he with him bears
'Gainst himself (ah me! I quake
'Gainst a king such charge to make)
But all must own,
The guilt is his and his alone.

CREON

(Str. 1)

Woe for sin of minds perverse,

Deadly fraught with mortal curse.

Behold us slain and slayers, all akin.

Woe for my counsel dire, conceived in sin.

Alas, my son,

Life scarce begun,

Thou wast undone.

The fault was mine, mine only, O my son!

CHORUS

Too late thou seemest to perceive the
    truth.

CREON

(Str. 2)

By sorrow schooled. Heavy the hand
    of God,

Thorny and rough the paths my feet have
    trod,

Humbled my pride, my pleasure turned to
    pain;

Poor mortals, how we labor all in vain!

[Enter SECOND MESSENGER]

SECOND MESSENGER

Sorrows are thine, my lord, and more to
     come,
One lying at thy feet, another yet
More grievous waits thee, when thou
     comest home.

CREON

What woe is lacking to my tale of woes?

SECOND MESSENGER

Thy wife, the mother of thy dead son here,
Lies stricken by a fresh inflicted blow.

CREON

(Ant. 1)
How bottomless the pit!
Does claim me too, O Death?
What is this word he saith,
This woeful messenger? Say, is it fit
To slay anew a man already slain?
Is Death at work again,
Stroke upon stroke, first son, then mother
     slain?

CHORUS

Look for thyself. She lies for all to view.

CREON

(Ant. 2)

Alas! another added woe I see.

What more remains to crown my agony?

A minute past I clasped a lifeless son,

And now another victim Death hath won.

Unhappy mother, most unhappy son!

SECOND MESSENGER

Beside the altar on a keen-edged sword

She fell and closed her eyes in night,
      but erst

She mourned for Megareus who
      nobly died

Long since, then for her son; with her last
      breath

She cursed thee, the slayer of her child.

CREON

(Str. 3)

I shudder with affright

O for a two-edged sword to slay outright

A wretch like me,

Made one with misery.

SECOND MESSENGER

'Tis true that thou wert charged by the
      dead Queen

As author of both deaths, hers and her
　　son's.

CREON
In what wise was her self-destruction
　　wrought?

SECOND MESSENGER
Hearing the loud lament above her son
With her own hand she stabbed herself to
　　the heart.

CREON
(Str. 4)
I am the guilty cause. I did the deed,
Thy murderer. Yea, I guilty plead.
My henchmen, lead me hence, away, away,
　　away,
A cipher, less than nothing; no delay!

CHORUS
Well said, if in disaster aught is well
His past endure demand the speediest
　　cure.

CREON
(Ant. 3)
Come, Fate, a friend at need,

Come with all speed!
Come, my best friend,
And speed my end!
Away, away!
Let me not look upon another day!

CHORUS
This for the morrow; to us are present
    needs
That they whom it concerns must take in
    hand.

CREON
I join your prayer that echoes my desire.

CHORUS
O pray not, prayers are idle; from
    the doom
Of fate for mortals refuge is there none.

CREON
(Ant. 4)
Away with me, a worthless wretch
    who slew
Unwitting thee, my son, thy mother too.
Whither to turn I know now; every way
Leads but astray,
And on my head I feel the heavy weight

Of crushing Fate.

CHORUS
Of happiness the chiefest part
Is a wise heart:
And to defraud the gods in aught
With peril's fraught.
Swelling words of high-flown might
Mightily the gods do smite.
Chastisement for errors past
Wisdom brings to age at last.

Made in the USA
Monee, IL
25 August 2022